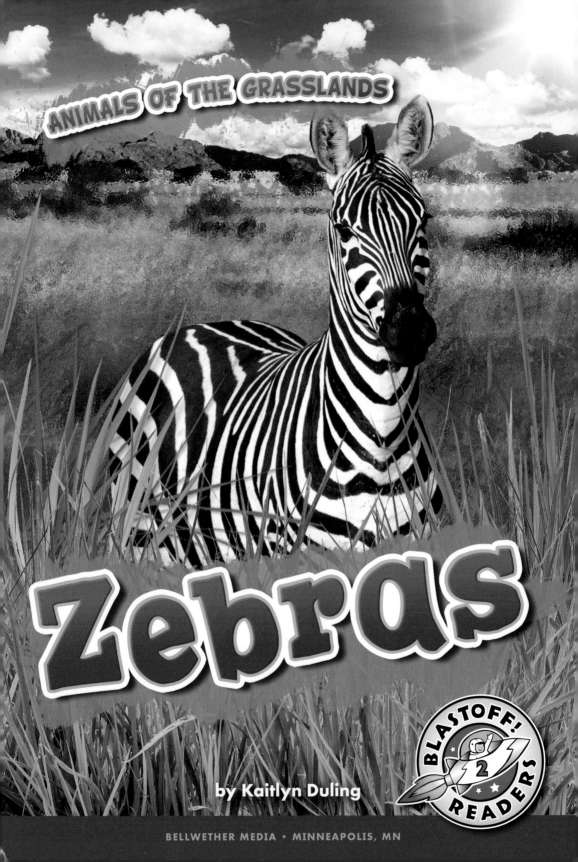

ANIMALS OF THE GRASSLANDS

Zebras

by Kaitlyn Duling

BLASTOFF!
2
READERS

BELLWETHER MEDIA • MINNEAPOLIS, MN

Note to Librarians, Teachers, and Parents:

Blastoff! Readers are carefully developed by literacy experts and combine standards-based content with developmentally appropriate text.

Level 1 provides the most support through repetition of high-frequency words, light text, predictable sentence patterns, and strong visual support.

Level 2 offers early readers a bit more challenge through varied simple sentences, increased text load, and less repetition of high-frequency words.

Level 3 advances early-fluent readers toward fluency through increased text and concept load, less reliance on visuals, longer sentences, and more literary language.

Level 4 builds reading stamina by providing more text per page, increased use of punctuation, greater variation in sentence patterns, and increasingly challenging vocabulary.

Level 5 encourages children to move from "learning to read" to "reading to learn" by providing even more text, varied writing styles, and less familiar topics.

Whichever book is right for your reader, Blastoff! Readers are the perfect books to build confidence and encourage a love of reading that will last a lifetime!

This edition first published in 2020 by Bellwether Media, Inc.

No part of this publication may be reproduced in whole or in part without written permission of the publisher. For information regarding permission, write to Bellwether Media, Inc., Attention: Permissions Department, 6012 Blue Circle Drive, Minnetonka, MN 55343.

Library of Congress Cataloging-in-Publication Data

Names: Duling, Kaitlyn, author.
Title: Zebras / by Kaitlyn Duling.
Description: Minneapolis, MN : Bellwether Media, Inc., [2020] | Series: Blastoff! Readers: Animals of the Grasslands | Includes bibliographical references and index. | Audience: Age 5-8. | Audience: K to Grade 3.
Identifiers: LCCN 2018061030 (print) | LCCN 2019001613 (ebook) | ISBN 9781618916372 (ebook) | ISBN 9781644870594 (hardcover : alk. paper)
Subjects: LCSH: Zebras--Juvenile literature.
Classification: LCC QL737.U62 (ebook) | LCC QL737.U62 D85 2020 (print) | DDC 599.665/7--dc23
LC record available at https://lccn.loc.gov/2018061030

Editor: Christina Leaf   Designer: Laura Sowers

Printed in the United States of America, North Mankato, MN.

Table of Contents

Life in the Grasslands

Zebras are **mammals** famous for their stripes. They live on the **savannas** of eastern Africa.

This grassland **biome** is hot and dry.

Plains Zebra Range

N
W ✦ E
S

range = ▢

Zebras have eyes on
either side of their heads.
They have strong
hearing, too.

These help them spot
predators on the grasslands.

Zebras have hard **hooves** and longs legs to run from predators.

hard hooves

Special Adaptations

eyes on the sides of their head

black and white stripes

hard hooves

The mammals can run up to 35 miles (56 kilometers) per hour!

Some predators get too close!

10

Zebra legs can deliver powerful kicks. Lions and other predators have to watch out.

Shoo, Flies!

Hot weather brings biting flies. Flies can carry disease.

Tails keep zebras safe. Zebras use their tails like fly swatters!

Plains Zebra Stats

Least Concern	Near Threatened	Vulnerable	Endangered	Critically Endangered	Extinct in the Wild	Extinct

conservation status: near threatened

life span: up to 25 years

13

Stripes keep flies away, too.
Flies do not like to land on them.

Each zebra has its own stripe **pattern**. These help zebras spot each other across the grassland.

Zebra Dinnertime

Zebras are **herbivores**. They have strong teeth for chewing plants.

Chewing wears down teeth. Luckily, zebra teeth never stop growing!

Zebra Diet

red oat grass

tanglehead

buffelgrass

migrating herd

Plants die in dry weather.
Zebras must **migrate** to find food.

They live and move across
the grasslands in **herds**.

Zebra herds migrate
with wildebeests. Zebras eat
tall grasses while wildebeests
eat short ones.

wildebeest

Zebras are team players.
They **adapt** to the grasslands
by working with others!

Glossary

adapt—to change over a long period of time

biome—a large area with certain plants, animals, and weather

herbivores—animals that only eat plants

herds—groups of zebras that live and travel together

hooves—the hard bottoms of some animals' feet

mammals—warm-blooded animals that have backbones and feed their young milk

migrate—to travel from one place to another, often with the seasons

pattern—a series of repeated designs

predators—animals that hunt other animals for food

savannas—flat grasslands with few trees

To Learn More

AT THE LIBRARY

Gagne, Tammy. *Zebras*. Lake Elmo, Minn.: Focus Readers, 2017.

Hansen, Grace. *Zebra*. Minneapolis, Minn.: Abdo, 2018.

Schuh, Mari. *Zebras*. Minneapolis, Minn.: Capstone Press, 2017.

ON THE WEB

FACTSURFER

Factsurfer.com gives you a safe, fun way to find more information.

1. Go to www.factsurfer.com.

2. Enter "zebras" into the search box and click 🔍.

3. Select your book cover to see a list of related web sites.

Index

The images in this book are reproduced through the courtesy of: Eugen Haag, front cover; GlobalP, pp. 4-5; pchoui, p. 6; 1001slide, pp. 6-7, 20-21; shaman1006, p. 8 (top); Kjetil Kolbjornsrud, pp. 8-9; Kimrawicz, p. 9; Parsenjit Mahata, pp. 10-11; Karel Bartik, p. 11; Richard Burn Photography, p. 12; Marc Guitard/ Getty Images, pp. 12-13; paula french, pp. 14-15; Michael Potter11, pp. 16-17; Susan Schmitz, p. 17 (left); Doikanoy, p. 17 (right); Macleay Grass Man/ Harry Rose/ Wikipedia, p. 17 (bottom); Tomás Guardia Bencomo, pp. 18-19; Delbars, p. 21; dmodlin01, p. 22.